What I've learned...

What I've learned...

◆

Thoughts from a Fire Chief

William C. Richmond

iUniverse, Inc.
New York Lincoln Shanghai

What I've learned...
Thoughts from a Fire Chief

iUniverse books may be ordered through booksellers or by contacting:

iUniverse
2021 Pine Lake Road, Suite 100
Lincoln, NE 68512
www.iuniverse.com
1-800-Authors (1-800-288-4677)

Because of the dynamic nature of the Internet, any Web addresses or links contained in this book may have changed since publication and may no longer be valid.

ISBN: 978-0-595-47006-8 (pbk)
ISBN: 978-0-595-91290-2 (ebk)

Printed in the United States of America

To the two primary constants in my life: my wife, E. J., and my daughter, Kelly. They aren't firefighters, but they know what it meant to me to be one. I love them both and I thank them for always being there for me …

And to Philadelphia firefighters of the past, present, and future. They just don't come any finer. Each of these groups has forged, or will forge, its own links of continued dedication and service into a chain of sterling performance and golden accomplishment that every Philadelphian has come to know, expect, rely on, and appreciate. This has been the case since March 15, 1871, and I'm sure it will continue to be so far into the future.

September 11, 2001 is long gone, but it will never be forgotten by those of us, however far removed, who share in the deep sorrow of that day. It is with profound and honored respect to the memory of the 343 New York City Firefighters who laid it all on the line that day I offer this special dedication.

Contents

Preface

It is a fair question to ask any writer the basis for his or her presumption that he or she is qualified to offer advice or guidance in a particular discipline. In the present case, a number of reasons could be offered in response to that query, but I will resort to only one. I served twenty-eight years in the Philadelphia Fire Department holding every rank from basic recruit to head of that department. I have responded to literally thousands of fires, ranging from grass along the highway to a building fire that went to twelve-and-a-half alarms. I have also experienced many fires where fatalities—one to eleven—have occurred. My credentials are that I have crawled the hallways, I have chipped ice off of my "running gear," and I have cried over fallen comrades. In short, I have been there.

What is presented here is a collection of thoughts, ideas, and concepts gathered over the years in our fire stations and on the firegrounds mentioned above. Much of my personal work philosophy as it relates to the fire service is included here as well. Some of it was costly to learn: mistakes we make often are. I'm not being critical, but I gained a great deal of knowledge by observing the questionable actions of others. Regardless of the source of this knowledge, it was all garnered entirely from real-life experience and not from textbooks or classrooms. This is not meant to demean formal education in any way, but rather to point out that we had our education in another school.

The reader may agree or disagree with the content of this book, and that's OK as it may stimulate discussion on the pros and cons of a particular item or issue. It is my view that the fire service can only benefit from such a debate. At any rate, this offering should be used as you, the reader, see fit. It's really only a collection of ideas, hints, suggestions, or reminders that just might prove helpful at some point in the reader's career. Browse through it when you have a spare moment or read it from cover to cover. Feel free to copy from it as you will. It is my hope, though, that everyone who picks it up will find at least one or two ideas that prove to be of value to him or her. If that turns out to be the case, I will consider the effort worthwhile.

Throughout this book the reader will be reminded of the worst day in the history of the American Fire Service: September 11, 2001. That date is referred to by the number 343 following each quote. This number, of course, refers to the NYFD firefighters who gave their hearts and souls that morning. They did what we all believe we would have done given the same circumstances. Many, many tributes have been paid to those brave men—this is mine.

Last, I have had a deep love for the fire service since my first day in fire school. Although there are days I would like to relive, by and large, I am satisfied that I have contributed something to that great institution. It is my sense that firefighters have a mystique about them that only other firefighters realize is there. It is, of course, the bond that ties people together who have intimately shared great joy, heartbreak, tribulation, and even terror. Since day one, I have worn a Maltese Cross—the international firefighter symbol—in the form of a Saint Florian medal around my neck, and I will continue to wear it until my last day. To me, it is not only a religious expression, but also a reminder of all that is right and good about our country, and I wear it proudly.

William C. Richmond

Leadership

Leadership is no mystery. It boils down to an unselfish and genuine concern for the troops, along with a full and complete understanding of the department's mission, and a working knowledge of its resources. Concern for the troops embraces not only their well-being, but their safety, training, and professional competence as well.

<343>

The department's Mission Statement should not only spell out services provided and address community concerns but should also serve as an action guide for your people.

<343>

Before accepting an appointment as the Chief, know in your mind and heart how far you will go when implementing or considering departmental economies. Draw your line in the sand even if that line is known only to you.

<343>

It's an old cliché that tells us, "You lead by example." Old though it may be, it's still the soundest approach to leadership.

<343>

The success of any fire department program depends on commitment. Commitment starts at the top and works its way down into the organization.

<343>

When you find an individual who combines leadership ability, management skills, and personal courage, you have the epitome and the ideal of a leader.

<343>

In the larger fire departments it is vitally important for the Chief to get out and meet the troops. Let your people put a face to your name by visiting them and by making yourself approachable. In the morning on your way into the office, stopping for coffee unannounced at your fire stations is a good way to learn what's really going on in the department. Make it understood early on, however, that you are not visiting with a critical eye.

<343>

In order to work things out or to plan ahead, you will need time for privacy, peace, and quiet, but the Chief must not let this become his or her work style. To communicate effectively, he or she has to get out and around.

<343>

Leadership doesn't always mean being in front; sometimes a leader does more good remaining in the background.

<343>

The Chief sets the standard and the example for the department, positive or negative, by everything he or she says, does, or even implies.

<343>

Firefighters know sincerity when they see or hear it, and they will respond in kind. By the same token, they will not respond to insincerity and are likely to dismiss it out of hand.

<343>

Of all the resources available to the Fire Chief, the most important is still those men and women who make up the department. Forgetting or overlooking this fact has been the downfall of many.

<343>

In working with his or her people, the "Golden Rule" is still a very good approach for the Chief to take.

<343>

If power or authority is not being used for good or for positive change, it is being misused.

<343>

There are four keys to success as a leader: work hard, be fair, listen and do what you feel is the right thing.

<343>

Autocratic leaders might succeed for a time, but in the long run, they will get only what they demand from their subordinates. Autocracy does not foster a cooperative attitude, and individuals will do only what they have to, contributing very little else under this type of leadership.

<343>

There are times when the best approach is to lighten up. Rely on your experience, knowledge, and training to tell you when those times are.

<343>

A leader accepts personal responsibility when things go wrong. By the same token, he or she passes the praise along to others when things go right.

<343>

The Chief's goals and objectives should be well-known to all. In the absence of this information, members of the organization are never quite sure what they are trying to accomplish or how they expect to get there.

<343>

Teamwork is built on trust, mutual respect, and the desire to achieve a common goal. Character is built by applying these traits in the face of adversity.

<343>

There is nothing wrong with admitting you made a mistake. On the contrary, owning up to mistakes is an action common to those who truly understand the essence of leadership.

<343>

If you accept the status quo, you're closing the door to departmental growth and development. Work to improve, strive for betterment, and look to tomorrow.

<343>

A good idea is a good idea no matter who came up with it. Embrace it, adopt it, use it, but give the full and proper credit to its originator.

<343>

Lack of appreciation undermines enthusiasm and motivation more than anything else can or will. If someone is doing a good job, tell him or her.

<343>

It takes high moral fiber and physical courage for a man or woman to continually extend himself or herself beyond normal limits, and that's exactly what we expect of our firefighters. Recognize this and praise or reward accordingly.

<343>

If you don't have the time to listen to what your people are trying to tell you, your priorities are out of line.

<343>

The lessons learned from our own operational mistakes, oversights, or shortcomings can be of great value to others. Admitting them sometimes takes courage, but sharing them is important.

<343>

Patience is an integral part of leadership. Even when things are not going well and the boss's patience is tested, there is never a valid reason for him or her to be discourteous or short with his or her people.

<343>

When you have the time to make a decision, take that time and use it well. When you don't, do what your training and experience tells you is right and move on.

<343>

Avoid knee-jerk reactions! Most issues or problems do not have to be resolved this moment. Sleep on it and it just may present an entirely different look in the morning.

<343>

Decisions made while angry or upset are often followed by regrets or second thoughts. Take a moment to cool down; then, and only then, decide.

<343>

In resolving major, difficult, or complex departmental issues, it is a sound idea to involve your command staff. They have a wealth of knowledge and practical experience that can be readily used. By not consulting them, you stand the chance of getting only marginal support.

<343>

Mistakes do not correct themselves. When you come across something that is not as it should be, see that it is corrected at the proper time and place. Remember, though, that the proper time is not always now and the proper place is not always here.

<343>

When the Chief presents a calm fireground demeanor, firefighters will respond in kind, and bystanders will have difficulty gauging just how bad a situation might be. We should be the last to contribute to the spread of panic or concern.

<343>

Fireground orders should be delivered in a calm and collected manner. Screaming or shouting has never been considered an effective means of communication.

<343>

Vulgarity might have its place in a locker room or military barracks, but it should not be used in public or in communicating between departmental members. Rough language does not make a firefighter.

<343>

The same approach to issuing orders will not be effective in all cases. Determine which managerial style an individual responds to, and use it.

<343>

The fireground is not the place for debate, but if one of your people has a bona fide objection to your planned course of action, listen to him or her.

<343>

In any public pronouncement regarding a successful fireground operation, the Chief should credit his or her firefighters first. Keep in mind that they did the work.

<343>

Complacency can be fatal. Take nothing for granted, and work constantly to keep both yourself and your department up-to-date. If we don't keep pace with what's going on around us, we're losing ground.

<343>

A yes-man never helped anyone. If you listen to one, do so at your own risk. In most cases, they are really only looking out for their own interests, not yours or the department's.

<343>

Once in a while take the time to sit back and let your imagination run free. Make an effort to think about what might be accomplished or what new horizons are out there to conquer. This is another form of long-range planning.

<343>

Don't assume!!! If you don't know for sure, find out.

<343>

Every Chief needs his or her "cabinet:" those trusted individuals he or she uses as a sounding board. They should be chosen carefully for their honesty and objectivity only. Don't tell me what you think I want to hear. Tell me how it really is or how you really feel about it.

<343>

If a firefighter dies or is seriously injured on duty, the Chief should see that his or her immediate family is treated as just that—immediate family.

<343>

If you asked me how to cope with the tremendous responsibility and pressure that goes with the Chief's job, I'd tell you to just do your best. Sounds simple, but I mean <u>really</u> do your best.

<343>

It is the Chief's responsibility to see that those who follow him or her are well prepared and fully qualified to assume command. Development of subordinates should be a personal priority for the Chief.

<343>

When you've left office, if you are remembered as a man or woman of character and kindness, you have been a success. This is a goal worth striving toward every day.

<343>

The acknowledgment of the need for a diverse work force starts at the top. It is up to the Chief to set the tone regarding race and gender within the department. The acceptable level for intolerance should be zero.

<343>

Backing up your decisions by offering your rationale will go a long way to gain you acceptance and support. It will also foster team building.

<343>

There is no doubt that the Fire Chief who is principled, approachable, and compassionate will also be respected.

<343>

The Fire Chief should use every opportunity to promote his or her department. If the Chief doesn't, who will?

<343>

In almost all cases, failure to delegate is an indication of insecurity in the "leader."

<343>

When giving orders or instructions make sure they are clear, concise and not subject to misinterpretation.

<343>

It is unhealthy to let a problem fester within an organization. Raise it, address it, resolve it, and put the matter behind you.

<343>

When misunderstandings occur in the course of business—and they will—face them head on. In this way, they will not grow out of proportion, and the organization will not suffer.

<343>

When assigning a task, a time frame for expected completion should be established as well as criteria for reporting. To assign a task and dismiss it from your mind is a formula for disaster. Following up is an essential element in any successful undertaking.

<343>

Make the objective or desired result clear, but leave the way it is achieved up to those assigned the task. You might be amazed at the ingenuity, creativity, and resourcefulness shown.

<343>

Breaking down a major project into smaller segments makes it a less formidable task. In many cases, it also allows us to involve more people at the same time.

<343>

A reprimand given in front of others reflects more negatively on the deliverer than on the recipient. It's a bad practice and is simply not necessary. Praise in public and chastise in private and you won't go wrong.

<343>

There must be at least one other person in the organization besides the Fire Chief who is up-to-date on all that is going on in the department. Your department is not the CIA, share what you know.

<343>

An open-door policy was never intended to replace or be used to circumvent the chain of command. It should be utilized only under extreme circumstances or unusual conditions.

<343>

Establishing cordial but businesslike working relationships with other department heads in city government should be on any new Fire Chief's early agenda.

<343>

An annual off-site retreat for the Fire Chief and his or her command provides the opportunity to encourage organizational growth. A change in environment can often change perspective as well, and an informal setting fosters participation.

<343>

When interpersonal relationships are based on integrity, good intent and candor, they are on solid ground.

<343>

Internal organizational conflict, when it rears its head, should never be aired in public. Nothing will erode public confidence in the department faster than the appearance of dissension in the ranks.

<343>

There is nothing more discouraging to an employee than not knowing how he or she is doing in his or her work or where he or she stands with the boss. Do all you can to see that this doesn't happen in your organization, regardless of its size. Periodic performance evaluations can help.

<343>

A strong factor in assuring complete integration of EMS and fire suppression within the department is the full and active support of the Chief.

<343>

It is worthy to consider that when the Fire Chief arrives on the fire-ground, he or she should assume command. As the Fire Chief is ultimately responsible for all that happens, they should also make the decisions. The Chief's role is to lead, not observe.

<343>

When the Chief elects not to use his or her seat belt responding to alarms or fails to wear full protective gear on the emergency scene, it sends the wrong message. "Do as I say, not as I do" just doesn't cut it.

<343>

The Fire Chief should determine at what level in the emergency operation he or she will respond. A big part of subordinate development takes place prior to his or her arrival. As an approach to providing command experience and to provide the opportunity for subordinates to develop practical operational knowledge, you might consider delaying your arrival on the fireground. If you now respond on the first alarm, wait until the second alarm, and so on.

<343>

Every complaint from the public should be acknowledged and investigated, and the results or final disposition shared with the complainant. This is how credibility is established and maintained.

<343>

Even in the face of deep disagreement, dialogue should never be abandoned. Find common ground and keep talking.

<343>

If we disagree, let's talk. If we don't see eye to eye, convince me or make me convince you. In any case, let's both listen and at least consider each other's point of view. Labor disputes might lead to litigation, but do all you can to settle the issue before that is needed.

<343>

In those jurisdictions where high-rise buildings are not required to have sprinkler systems, the Fire Chief has his or her legislative agenda already set. The same holds true for residential smoke detectors. Nothing will do more to prevent loss of life than sprinkler systems coupled with early warning.

<343>

In my view firefighters are still the most respected public servants. We are still looked up to by our neighbors and friends, still turned to in times of distress, and still considered role models for the young. Let's do what we can to keep it that way!

<343>

The common thread that runs through the fabric of morale is pride—pride in oneself, pride in one's unit, and pride in the department. Departmental pride should be at the top of the Fire Chief's to-do list.

<343>

Morale is one of those things you can neither see nor feel, and it's either there or it isn't. When it's there you can soar; when it's not, you will only be going through the motions.

<343>

You should always be willing to "sign" your work product. That is, put your name on what you have done, be it a written report or a fireground operation.

<343>

Pity the Fire Chief who sees no need for an employee assistance program. He or she is either not paying attention or operating in dreamland.

<343>

There is really only one occasion that merits the giving of unsolicited advice. That occasion is when it is the last step before disciplinary action.

<343>

In labor relations, not every issue is worth going to war over. Keep in mind, though, that some battles are certainly important enough to fight. You must know and understand the difference.

<343>

An old boss once told me, "The stronger the influence to do right throughout the organization's leadership, the less of a problem you have." The influence he is talking about is you, the Fire Chief.

<343>

Management

Department members must know and understand that gender or racial intolerance is simply not acceptable. Violations of the department's policies regarding tolerance should be handled swiftly, strongly, and consistently.

<343>

In dealing promptly, fairly, and consistently in disciplinary matters, you will considerably lighten your workload in this area.

<343>

Asking questions is a sound management approach. The answers you get will often surprise you—sometimes pleasantly and sometimes not so pleasantly.

<343>

Continually examine what you do, why you do it, how you do it, who does it and what it costs. The answer to those questions just might lead to a better way of doing business. In addition, you might find you are doing things you shouldn't and not doing things you should.

<343>

Delegation is the all-purpose tool that lets us get much more done than we could have otherwise. It also goes a long way in the development of subordinates.

<343>

It is important that support staff be instilled with the same sense of mission as the troops in the field. Both must depend a great deal on each other if departmental goals are to be fully realized.

<343>

Management can be likened to juggling: any number of things can be going on at one time and attention must be paid to them all.

<343>

If you have an idea you're giving some thought to, float it unofficially. By gauging the response, you'll get an idea if it's worth pursuing, or whether it's worthwhile but in need of modification.

<343>

It's extremely important that you thoroughly understand your mission and responsibilities as well as your authority to carry them out. You can be challenged on any one of them at any given time.

<343>

"Unity of Command" simply means that we are quite clear for whom we work. Put another way, it also spells out who we should take our problems to first.

<343>

We know what we do. The thing to identify is what *more* can we do. There are many things you department can do for the community beyond EMS and firefighting. Seek out those opportunities.

<343>

A firefighter should have no doubt about what is expected of him or her. Departmental standards must be valid, current, clear, and uniformly applied to all.

<343>

The first thing to do when faced with a problem is to ask yourself one question: "Is it my problem?" If it's yours, handle it. If it's not, direct it to the proper office or individual.

<343>

Keep abreast of modern technology as it relates to the fire service. Thermal imaging cameras, integrated Self Contained Breathing Apparatus systems, Automatic External Defibrilators, computer programs and, a variety of other items are out there. Use them or at least learn about them.

<343>

Fire department organizational charts often have too many boxes. Simplify yours to the extent that you can still reflect the real organization. In most cases a fire department will have only three major branches: operations, fire prevention, and administration.

<343>

The community knows what emergency services it wants. If you don't know or are not sure what these are, ask them. Periodic surveys of those you serve can often produce interesting results and frequently suggest new programs.

<343>

NFPA and other nationally recognized standards can be valuable tools for the Fire Chief who must support his or her budget requests before local authoritative bodies. In addition, whether we like it or not, these documents have become the "standard of care" for our industry, and we can be called to task because of their content.

<343>

With very rare exceptions, one's immediate supervisor should be given the first shot at resolving any problem or concern you may have.

<343>

It is easy to become comfortable and complacent, so it could be helpful to bring in outsiders to take an objective look at your operation. This service is available through fire service organizations, the insurance industry, and the private sector and can prove to be an idea worthy of consideration.

<343>

There should be a clear and unambiguous organizational path from the newest firefighter in the department right up to the Fire Chief. Everyone should know for whom they work. Everyone should also know what and who they are responsible for.

<343>

"Span of Control" is a basic managerial precept designed to assure realistic distribution of supervisory responsibility. There is no question that there are limitations on how many individuals one person can effectively supervise. Much depends, of course, on the nature of the work.

<343>

The expedient solution to a problem frequently turns out to be the most costly in the long run, not only in terms of dollars, but also in terms of the precedent we are setting. When contemplating a managerial decision, a good question to ask is: "Am I setting a precedent here, and if so, can I live with it?

<343>

There are times when your decision will be to take no action. That's OK; just be sure you've carefully weighed your other options.

<343>

A fine line distinguishes debate, argument, and strong objection from insubordination. The line is there nonetheless and should never be crossed.

<343>

Discipline and documentation are like Siamese twins: one cannot go anywhere without the other.

<343>

The administration of discipline is never a pleasant task, but, when called for, it is essential to the well-being of the organization that it be doled out promptly, fairly, and consistently.

<343>

Formally recognizing outstanding performance should be an integral part of every fire department's personnel action program. Consider an annual awards day as a vehicle for accomplishing this. An individual's family can then share in the glory of his or her achievement or accomplishment.

<343>

Standard operating procedures are the instruments through which uniform guidelines translate into uniform performance.

<343>

Operating any business, including a fire department, without a system of quality assurance will eventually lead to trouble—trouble that can easily be avoided by continually monitoring all aspects of your department's activities.

<343>

If your schedule is always full and you can't find time for other things you feel you should be doing, it's a good bet you're not delegating enough.

<343>

Documentation is the wheel that drives all successful personnel actions. This is true in disciplinary matters as well as the more positive activities.

<343>

As a rule, decision making should be done at the lowest level in the organization that has all the facts as well as the authority to make that decision. However, the chain of command should be made aware of decisions made.

<343>

Line is line and staff is staff, but we are all part of the same fire department and have the same overall mission to accomplish. There has to be departmental machinery in place that facilitates the exchange of information and viewpoints between these two entities. Periodic meetings can help.

<343>

In planning, all options or alternatives to the issue at hand should be identified when possible. Those that you deem valid should then be explored to a reasonable conclusion.

<343>

Whether you use "Management by Objectives" or some other method, establishing goals can be a very positive influence for individual as well as departmental development.

<343>

Left on its own, your span of control can develop an uncanny ability to expand and grow. For your own survival, keep it under control and manageable by structuring organizational relationships well.

<343>

It is good practice to include representatives from all ranks on departmental committees. Doing so provides access to a world of invaluable firsthand experience.

<343>

The Chief who fails to plan is certainly going to play catch-up. He or she will always be at least on step behind.

<343>

Information not shared has been the downfall of many an operation or project. Those who should know must know.

<343>

If your staff is not comprised of people with proven ability or potential, you're working with a handicap. Seek out those in the department with the qualities and commitment that can enhance or further the department's mission and consider them for staff assignments.

<343>

If your present organizational structure is not working or not working well—change it.

<343>

A check list is more than a crutch. It is an invaluable tool in seeing that details are accomplished and responsibilities met. Relying solely on your memory is a trap to be avoided.

<343>

The Fire Chief should hold frequent and regularly scheduled meetings with all those who play a role in running the department. This not only includes line and staff managers, but, at times, also includes representatives of the department's bargaining unit. These groups don't have to meet together, but meetings should be held nonetheless.

<343>

Your organizational Mission Statement should be boldly printed and posted on every bulletin board and hung on every office wall in the department. Further, each member should be issued a personal copy for ready reference.

<343>

A meeting should run like a railroad. It should start on time and reach its destination on time, and everyone present should have a good idea of where they're going and what they can expect along the way.

<343>

Substandard performance in an otherwise good employee is symptomatic of a deeper problem. It's in everyone's best interest to find out what that problem is and to seek a resolution.

<343>

Many Fire Chiefs have benefited from the work product of departmental standing committees. Committees make an excellent vehicle by which to tap institutional knowledge and experience, and also give others a stake in the department's growth.

<343>

In today's times, networking is not a luxury or a hobby, it is vitally important. It offers us a way to find out how the other guy is doing things and why. There are many ways to do this in the fire service, and it is a wise Fire Chief who seeks out those opportunities.

<343>

Generally accepted national standards provide a road map for today's Fire Chief and they offer support and justification in some cases and can be of value should litigation arise.

<343>

Coming in an hour early and staying an hour late once or twice a week can provide the time to not only catch up, but also to be somewhat creative as well. Extra time is a little luxury we should all give ourselves.

<343>

Every Chief's best friend should be the three-by-five card or its electronic equivalent, the PDA. The only sure way to remember anything is to write it down or record it in some fashion while it's fresh. In addition, the everyday demands on the Fire Chief's time can be exhausting. His or her computer or PDA could be the answer he or she needs.

<343>

Talent, imagination, and vision can be found in every organization. It is worth every effort you might extend to identify them, access them, and harness them for the good of the department.

<343>

"Management by Walking Around" is ideally suited for fire service managers. Stopping by another' person's work place can facilitate the healthy exchange of ideas and information in an informal setting.

<343>

Feedback to a manager is like rain to a flower or plant because it is vital for continued growth. Without feedback, we have no idea how things are really going.

<343>

Departmental directives, orders, and procedures should be flexible enough to allow discretion when discretion is called for. Every circumstance can't possibly be covered in writing, so it is imperative that latitude be worked into the process.

<343>

Your organizational chart should be as simple and as basic as you can make it, but still leave no doubt as to who reports to whom.

<343>

Fire departments are uniquely equipped to provide non-emergency services beyond their stated mission. Those services carry with them the potential to provide greater community service and even generate revenue in some cases. Consideration should be given to providing them, resources permitting.

<343>

For the most part fire responses are down across the country while EMS incidents are up. Providing emergency medical services is a grand productivity enhancement for a fire department and frequently supports or justifies staffing levels.

<343>

Our client is the community, and we must do all we can to provide the level and type of service it identifies as important to it. If you're not sure what or how important those services are—ask.

<343>

You must use the legislative process in your local jurisdiction to ensure a more fire-safe community. Learn how it works and how to use it effectively.

<343>

In times when money is tight, regional cooperation or concepts should be vigorously explored. There is much that can be done working with surrounding communities that we can't do on our own.

<343>

The use of "acting" officers is an excellent tool for personal and career development. In many cases, it can save money as well. This is a win/win arrangement.

<343>

Your data-management system should capture all the information you need to operate effectively. It can act as a guidepost in assessing where you have been, what you are doing now, and where you should be going. A well-thought-out management information system will eventually pay for itself by aiding you in the optimum distribution and utilization of your resources.

<343>

Your organization's "number crunchers" can tell you a great deal about what's going on within the department. Never underestimate their ability to do so. You must, however, let them know what you need to know.

<343>

In preparing the department's budget, be realistic, but ask for what you need. At the same time, you must support your requests with solid documentation.

<343>

With the influx of packaged fire service management computer programs, there is simply no excuse for any fire department to continue using word of mouth, ledgers, or typewriters to manage their information.

<343>

Data isn't everything, but its thoughtful evaluation and use is the key to many sound management decisions.

<343>

There is no question that seniority is important, but it should not be the sole basis for personnel decisions. Just because someone has been around the longest does not mean he or she is the most qualified either for promotion or for a particular assignment.

<343>

Making work assignments on the basis of an individual's special talents instead of on the position's actual job requirements may be OK in the short run, but how will it play out when that individual leaves or is replaced?

<343>

The importance of comparing national fire service statistics is that they give us a rough idea of how we've been doing. They only provide a rough comparison, however, because no two fire departments or jurisdictions are exactly alike.

<343>

Comparing your departmental resources and workload with similar jurisdictions can provide supportive ammunition in budget presentations or like situations.

<343>

The periodic rotation of company officers provides an excellent opportunity for them to develop and broaden their work experience and geographic familiarity.

<343>

A good quality assurance program ensures high performance standards. It can also validate our strengths and weaknesses.

<343>

A fire department that is not providing EMS to the community it serves should examine their reason why this is so.

<343>

The threat of terrorism is going to be with us for a long time. Recognize this and make sure your department is prepared in terms of resources and training.

<343>

We must provide for the mitigation of Haz Mat incidents within our local boundaries in some way. If we can't do it ourselves, we must seek an alternative provider. Regionalization works well in these situations.

<343>

If your Mission Statement includes the saving of lives, providing EMS is an excellent way to start. There is an EMS delivery system model that will fit your department and your community. Seek it out and adopt it.

<343>

A system of periodically rotating personnel through staff positions can go a long way in shaping a well-balanced officer cadre. At the same time, it broadens the individual's experience and makes them even more valuable to the organization.

<343>

However improbable it might seem, a mass casualty event is possible in every community. It behooves us then to prepare as best we can for that possibility.

<343>

A realistic and systematic apparatus replacement schedule or program should be part of the ongoing agenda of every Fire Chief. Purchasing by crisis can be crippling, and city fathers must be made to realize this.

<343>

Each of our fire stations should have adequate supplies on hand to see assigned units through the early stages of a major disaster.

<343>

There is no community that does not, at one time or another, have the need for technical rescue. We must either provide it ourselves or arrange for it through others.

<343>

There is nothing wrong with an individual wearing "two hats" as long as he or she can devote adequate time and resources to each, and one does not negatively impact on the other. This is particularly critical in the operations arena.

<343>

A manager or supervisor may have many skills, but reading minds might not be one of them. Keep him or her informed, make him or her aware of troublesome issues, and be sure the lines of communication stay open.

<343>

Promoting AED installation and training throughout the community is an effective way to support our own EMS effort. Shopping malls, theaters, restaurants, transportation terminals, churches, and gated communities are just a few examples of the many places these units can be located to assist us.

<343>

Fire departments work for the community and will ultimately do what the public wants them to do. At the present, EMS is a priority neighborhood concern, and it behooves us to listen.

<343>

Providing quality, and complete protective gear is the responsibility of the Fire Chief. It is the responsibility of all ranks to see that it's worn and that it's worn properly.

<343>

If your people are not using all their protective gear and equipment on the fireground, you're the problem.

<343>

If an individual physical-fitness plan is not part of your department's overall program, perhaps it should be. It is an excellent way to prepare firefighters to meet the oftentimes exhausting demands they face on the fireground. A well-planned tour of duty should include mental as well as physical activity.

<343>

Spending time and money on officer development is an intelligent investment of departmental resources. Future dividends reaped will validate that investment.

<343>

History has shown us that nothing can be more embarrassing to a city administration than a badly handled major emergency event. Anticipation, planning, and preparedness are how this embarrassment is prevented.

<343>

If you want the press and the public to have a better understanding of what you do, invite them into the fire stations to view the apparatus and to observe your training activities. This is a solid way to garner their support for those future issues that might be important to you and in which they could help.

<343>

There should be no doubt in the public's mind how to reach you when it needs to—either for emergencies or for other problems. Always strive to keep that information in front of the community.

<343>

If our fire stations do not have smoke detectors, what kind of a message are we sending to the community?

<343>

Where maintenance standards are high, replacement needs and costs will be correspondingly low.

<343>

When preparing departmental apparatus and equipment specifications, it's a good idea to utilize the practical experience of those most familiar with the subject—your firefighters.

<343>

If apparatus maintenance is neglected, you might pay dearly for it, on the fireground, for instance. A preventive maintenance program is a must, not an option.

<343>

Putting off needed station repairs while addressing present budget problems only adds to their eventual cost. A scheduled preventive building maintenance program that is adhered to is the answer.

<343>

Whenever possible, include room to grow in the design of new fire stations. This gives you more flexibility in any future movement and/or relocation of apparatus or units.

<343>

In the planning process of designing a new fire station or remodeling an older one, you should include those that will be using the facility in that process.

<343>

In the providing of protective clothing for both the street and the station, look to the NFPA Standards.

<343>

Growth and development in our community must be continually monitored. It is our responsibility to anticipate and adjust to population, occupancy, and construction changes in order to provide the proper level of fire protection and emergency services. Adequate water supply should be a major consideration.

<343>

Firefighting is a business in which workers have no guarantee that they will return home safely—or even return home at all. So always keep firefighter safety in mind.

<343>

If I don't know what to do next, I could be in trouble. If I don't know where to find out what to do next, I'm in trouble for sure.

<343>

In most cases, a firefighter who stumbles or falters in his or her off-duty life because of substance abuse is entitled to a second chance—but only one.

<343>

Unfortunately, firefighters, whether volunteer or paid, are all burdened with the same responsibilities in safeguarding their communities. Therefore, they each must make every effort to cope with the ever-increasing demands placed on them by a host of outside agencies. Their respective communities should be kept aware of those responsibilities.

<343>

However much we dislike it, there's no question that substance abuse among our firefighters is a reality. Face it, address it, and work to eliminate it, but do not accept or tolerate it.

<343>

The Chief who is not computer literate is missing out on one of today's finest management tools. If you fall into this category, do something about it today.

<343>

Periodic physical examinations for active firefighters and EMS personnel are an investment we can't afford to overlook. Everybody wins: those we serve, the department, and the individual firefighter or emergency medical worker.

<343>

When changes come to your department and you're not happy about them, remember the dinosaurs. (They're not around anymore.) One thing you can always count on is that there will be change.

<343>

The road to promotion in the fire department must be open to all. The map showing firefighters how to get there has to be clear as well. The actual trip, however, is up to the individual.

<343>

You've heard it before: "The chain of command is only as strong as its weakness link." Don't let yourself or your subordinates become the link that fails.

<343>

Operations

A valuable asset for the Fire Chief, and a skill that should be worked on, is the ability to quickly adjust to rapidly deteriorating fireground conditions. Flexibility and the ability to adapt are the very cornerstones of successful fireground operations.

<343>

Operating without a formal Incident Command System is no longer an option. It must be a fact of life in these litigious times. In the past, the Chief ran the whole fire operation in his or her head. It's just too complex now for that system to work effectively. A well-thought-out Incident Command System is the answer.

<343>

Never respond from the station without a clear idea of where you're going, how you're going to get there, and what your assigned location is on the fireground.

<343>

If your Incident Command System is used regularly on smaller events, department members will become comfortable with it and better prepared when the bigger ones come.

<343>

A clear understanding in your own mind of what you're trying to accomplish on the fireground is essential. Letting those who will carry out the necessary tasks also know is vital to a successful operation. Share what you're thinking with them.

<343>

There are times when you are unable to complete a given assignment, order, or instruction for any number of valid reasons. That can happen, but make sure the individual who gave you the original order is informed, as other critical activities might be depending on it.

<343>

If you don't understand or are unclear about a fireground order, speak up. The Chief will respect your honesty, and the operation will stand a much better chance of succeeding.

<343>

Primary searches are frequently made in extremely adverse conditions, which only goes to underscore the importance of a complete and thorough secondary search.

<343>

"Size-Up" is not a one-time thing. It's a continual and ongoing process. Things can happen fast on the fireground, so we must pay attention. The important thing about "Size-Up" procedures is to have one. Develop a system you're comfortable with and use it, or adopt one of those available.

<343>

Regarding accountability, one way or another the Chief should always know who is on the fireground and what they are doing.

<343>

The "Walk Around" or "360-degree tour" is an extremely important component of the incident commander's size-up and should be done as quickly as possible. Getting the "Big Picture" early on can save a lot of grief down the road.

<343>

The incident commander has only two eyes and can't see all that is going on. He or she would be a fool not to use the eyes of others on the fireground. This idea also stresses the importance of periodic reporting from all sectors.

<343>

Inherent in a sector commander's assignment is the responsibility to ensure the safety of firefighters working with him or her and to keep the incident commander completely and regularly informed of conditions.

<343>

For all intents and purposes, the fire building involved belongs to the fire department until the operation is complete, up to and including the post-fire investigation—or even longer if that is deemed necessary.

<343>

On many fire or other emergency scenes, we are temporarily responsible for the property and personal possessions of others. It's a good practice to see that they are watched over with care. Moreover, it's our job to do so.

<343>

If the first arriving units do not place their apparatus properly and prudently, it's often too late and the operation stands a good chance of turning into a fiasco. There are few things more difficult than moving engines and ladders once they're placed in service.

<343>

It is important not to underestimate the size of initial hose lines used. When in doubt, opt for the larger. You can always break down and use a smaller size hose later.

<343>

When ordering hose lines stretched, consider the time it takes to get them in place. There is no quick way to accomplish this task, so you must anticipate your needs.

<343>

When you need help on the fireground, call for it. Nothing is more frustrating than trying to do too much with too little, and you can always return equipment or send back personnel if they are not needed. It's time to think about calling for help when you have little or nothing left in reserve on the fireground.

<343>

Make sure you and your people know about all available water sources in the community. There's no telling when they might be needed. In addition, those areas in the community that present water supply problems should be identified, and action taken to correct those situations.

<343>

When a change in conditions—structural or otherwise—occurs in a building in which there is a fire that you don't understand or can't explain, it's sound practice to evacuate your firefighters until you determine what caused that change.

<343>

Rescue does not end once the people are out of a building. Ask yourself, "Where are we going to put these people?" and "Who will address their future personal needs?" You can't just evacuate occupants and then let them stand out in the weather with no idea of what comes next. It is up to the incident commander to see that provisions are made for the continued care of those removed from their homes or businesses.

<343>

When you've called for help from the fireground or emergency scene, know where you are going to place it or what you are going to do with it. If there is any question in your mind, set up a staging area and draw help from there.

<343>

An effective accountability system must be in place and used. This small investment in time can mean the difference between life and death for your firefighters. The history of the American fire service includes too many tragic stories that could have turned out differently given an effective accountability system.

<343>

In dealing with hazardous materials, if you're not sure what you are dealing with or if you are unable to identify what it is, assume the worst.

<343>

After rescues have been accomplished, exposures and possible extension of the fire should be your primary concerns. Remember also, that at that point, you are now dealing with "real estate," not people, and the degree of risk taken measured accordingly.

<343>

When fighting structure fires, keep in mind the six possible directions the fire can travel, and watch them all closely and continually.

<343>

A Rapid Intervention Team (RIT) is not a luxury on the fireground. It has a specific purpose for being there that demands proper accommodation.

<343>

In times of extreme weather, rotation of personnel on the fireground should be an early consideration.

<343>

Whether we agree or not, the "Two In/Two Out" rule was designed and created to protect firefighters. It was never intended, however, to delay or deter fireground rescues.

<343>

Salvage and overhaul are two fireground activities that never seem to get the credit they rightfully deserve. You can save the owner or occupant a great deal of distress and limit the overall damage by doing these jobs vigorously.

<343>

If firefighters are not critically debriefed when that need is identified, the operation that necessitated it is not over. The need will depend on the extent of mental anguish the event may have caused.

<343>

Always do your very best so you never leave a fireground feeling there was something more you could have or should have done.

<343>

Every fire should be critiqued, if only in your own mind. Lessons learned can prove useful to you and to others on future firegrounds.

<343>

"Rekindles" happen. Just make sure they don't happen on your watch. Take all the time you need to see that the fire is completely out—even to the extent of setting up a fire watch.

<343>

When you are debating whether or not to call for additional help, do it. Your doubt is reason enough.

<343>

Second effort on the football field gains extra yards. Second effort in a hot and smoky hallway can save lives.

<343>

If you as the Fire Chief arrive on the fireground and find yourself uncomfortable with the placement of personnel and apparatus or the strategy being used, do something about it.

<343>

When responding to an alarm, remember that lights and sirens do not make you invulnerable or accident-proof. Drive carefully!

<343>

The potential for building failure or collapse is present on almost all firegrounds. Know, understand, and heed the early warning signs, and then take the appropriate precautionary action.

<343>

"How do I get out of here in a hurry if I have to?" This is a question every firefighter should always keep in the back of his or her mind. The primary escape route may no longer be available so secondary escape routes should be explored or identified.

<343>

The use of safety guidelines or ropes during complex search operations should be a given. It's easy to get disoriented in fire conditions, and guidelines can quickly become lifelines.

<343>

When working on a roof, identify and establish your escape route. It's easy to get distracted in the heat of firefighting, so from time to time check to make sure your path off that roof is open and clear.

<343>

A breathing apparatus is designed to make sure you are doing just that after your firefighting days are over. If smoke is present, put your SCBA on. Products of combustion can kill. Where there's smoke, there's need for a breathing apparatus. This holds true during the overhaul stage of the fire as well.

<343>

Intersection accidents have proven extremely costly to firefighters. Apply your brakes when approaching intersections, and check all oncoming traffic lanes. The ultimate method of preventing accidents is to have your vehicle under control at all times.

<343>

An unsecured portable ladder is an accident waiting to happen. The same holds true for suctions or other appliances that are not lashed down.

<343>

When you reach for a power tool, reach for your eye protection at the same time.

<343>

Keep in touch! Good fireground communication is vital to any operational success you might have. Given the present state of communication equipment, there is no reason not to be in close contact with everyone operating on the fireground.

<343>

Counter theories not withstanding, the best policy is to dispatch the closest available units to fire or medical emergencies. This holds true for the crossing of jurisdictional or political boundaries as well, and is one important reason we have mutual and automatic aid agreements in the first place.

<343>

Fireground safety is important enough to dedicate an individual to that singular task. His or her only concern on the fireground should be safety, and he or she should be invested with the authority to take immediate, corrective action.

<343>

The placement of standards or outriggers should be done very carefully; footing must be firm, and overhead wires avoided. In the winter, make sure you remove any ice or snow before lowering them.

<343>

Fireground safety is not only the responsibility of departmental leadership but of the individual firefighter as well. Wearing full protective gear is a good first step toward safety.

<343>

When operating on a large or complex fireground, the value of communications takes on even greater importance. Periodic reporting is a good first step in acknowledging that importance.

<343>

To get help on the way, all a dispatcher really needs to know is what and where. Additional information can and should be gathered and then given to responding units as it is obtained.

<343>

There is always time, even on the fireground, to brief the press. They have a right to know, and you have a responsibility to tell them. However, you set the time and terms.

<343>

Preplanning often provides the early warning that things are not always as they appear. The last thing you need on any fireground is a surprise. Large buildings and other target hazards should be identified and preplanned.

<343>

Adequate documentation during post-fire investigations can save a lot of trouble down the road. That is, when and if the case goes to court or when the private-sector fire investigators arrive.

<343>

Thermal imaging cameras are no longer in the trial stage. They are a proven commodity and a vital addition to the equipment inventory of any fire department.

<343>

When jockeying portable ladders on an emergency scene, pay attention to the many existing hazards: overhead electrical wires, for instance. Firefighters have been lost and seriously injured performing this task.

<343>

Firefighters are not police officers. Police work should be left to those properly trained and equipped to perform that function.

<343>

No two fires are ever alike. They may share common features, but that's where it ends. There are so many variables in fire development that we must be always on the alert for the differences.

<343>

The fireground command post should be set up so the Incident Commander is in a position to see as much as he or she can and still be accessible.

<343>

"Surround and Drown" may be an old cliché, but there are times when it is the safest and soundest way to approach a fire.

<343>

In today's world every fire department should have a procedure in place to address bomb situations—suspected or confirmed.

<343>

During multiagency operations, a single departmental individual should coordinate and direct his or her people and their activities. He or she should have the authority to make necessary decisions.

<343>

The ten-minute interval for fireground reporting established by the NFPA is a sensible approach that should be followed on all fire scenes regardless of size.

<343>

There is no time for freelancing on emergency scenes. Those in supervisory positions must maintain tight control over the activities of the personnel for whom they are responsible.

<343>

Training

Training just for training's sake is a questionable practice. Clear, relevant, and timely topics should be the order of the day.

<343>

A firefighter's job can be made only so safe by technology or procedural mandates. Training, experience, and knowledge are still as important now as they ever were.

<343>

The first place and the very worst place that inadequate training rears its head is on the fireground. Repetition of engine and ladder practices before the fact is the most practical way to ensure efficient fireground performance when it is really needed.

<343>

The better trained an individual or unit is, the less close supervision or scrutiny needed.

<343>

Multi-unit drills are like preseason football games. They provide the opportunity to correct what's wrong without counting for too much.

<343>

If we expect company officers to be capable first-line trainers, we must adequately prepare them for that role.

<343>

The only true way to gain ease and familiarity in the raising of ladders, all kinds and sizes, is by raising them repeatedly. At the same time, their capabilities and limitations become apparent.

<343>

In the absence of a significant work load, training in the basics becomes even more important. Skills can easily deteriorate or be lost through inactivity.

<343>

A few hours invested in computer training within the organization will pay for itself quickly, and it will be time well spent.

<343>

Well-thought-out tactical training at all levels of the organization will pay dividends on future firegrounds. There are a host of simulation programs out there worthy of being absorbed into your overall training program.

<343>

In the absence of an in-place departmental requirement for formal or continuing education, start your own program and encourage those around you to do the same. Education in all its forms can only benefit the department.

<343>

We should all know how to properly and safely operate every tool, appliance, or piece of equipment carried on our rig. If we don't know how to use it before it's needed, it's too late to learn once you're on the fireground.

<343>

No training on the handling of hazardous materials is ever wasted. The potential for a major hazmat event exists in every community that has a river, a railway system, an airport, or a major roadway passing through it. Every jurisdiction has its vulnerabilities in terms of potential disasters. Identify those vulnerabilities in your community and seek to address them.

<343>

Drilling on the tactical use of standpipes will prepare firefighters for the day or night they have to actually use one—and rest assured, that time will come.

<343>

Examine your driver-training program with an eye to the realization that not every firefighter should be driving emergency response vehicles. Every firefighter should be schooled in safe and sound driving principles, however, as they may be called upon to use driving skills in an emergency.

<343>

The role of tabletop exercises in community-integrated emergency management should not be taken lightly. There is no substitute for prior training when a real emergency hits.

<343>

The only way to ensure truly integrated emergency management in the community is to train in this specific discipline long before an emergency occurs. Because of our lead role in this activity, we can play a big part in convincing city fathers that this is so.

<343>

Fire Prevention

A completely successful fire department is one that responds to no fires. However improbable that is, your fire-prevention program should have that end as its goal.

<343>

Your community's exposure to life risk and potential property damage from fire can never be totally eliminated, but that's not to say you shouldn't keep trying.

<343>

The truth is that when fire suppression is needed, we have all failed to some extent. The problem might have been that our fire prevention messages were either ignored, misunderstood, or missed by the community.

<343>

All our department resources should be directed toward assisting the "Tip Man" in doing his or her job. Equally important is the direction of our resources toward not making the man or woman on the end of the hose line's job necessary in the first place. Fire prevention is the best way to do that.

<343>

The essence of fire prevention is education, inspection, and enforcement. These truly are the "Big Three."

<343>

Inspections and code enforcement complement each other. You really can't have one without the other. In some cases, inspections lead to enforcement, and aggressive code enforcement is an excellent place to start in making your community fire safe.

<343>

Using fire suppression forces for inspection activities makes good sense. We get to know the community, and they get to know us, and we may even prevent future emergencies in the process. If your department is not doing company inspections, you are missing out on an opportunity to learn firsthand what's out there and to educate the public at the same time.

<343>

Reviewing plans gets you in on the ground floor and helps you determine the nature of your future playing field. The more information you have before hand, the better.

<343>

The benefits realized from fire prevention activities are difficult to quantify, but they are there nonetheless.

<343>

The public has to know and understand its role and responsibility in lowering the fire risk in the community. It's our role and responsibility to see that they understand that responsibility.

<343>

"Target Hazards" should be given the attention their special status deserves. You can't know too much about a property or occupancy in this category.

<343>

In many ways, post-fire investigations can point toward the way your fire prevention unit should travel.

<343>

General

In accomplishing your departmental mission, don't look for an easier way, look for a better way.

<343>

When working in emergency situations that do not fit nicely into your standard operating procedures, do what you think is right at the moment; the rest can be sorted out in the morning.

<343>

The future comes one day at a time and we should welcome it, but to keep pace with the future you must continually grow with it. Keep yourself abreast of what's going on in the fire service, as well as in the community you serve.

<343>

The important thing about decision-making is that you use a structured and systematic approach. The particular method or procedure you use to get there is really only secondary.

<343>

Before you take a problem to the boss make sure you can also offer him or her a place to start in resolving it. This can take the form of a firm recommendation or a number of well-thought-out options.

<343>

One of the biggest mistakes you can make in life is to assume the other guy or girl looks at things the same way you do. It isn't always so!

<343>

It is counter-productive and a terrible waste of time to revisit or dwell on questionable past decisions. Take the lessons you have learned, and do all you can to avoid repeating them.

<343>

When faced with a situation not covered by written policy, call to mind the department's Mission Statement and make your decision consistent with that mandate.

<343>

The satisfaction that comes from firefighting is in knowing we have been tried, tested, and had the ability, knowledge, and courage to prevail.

<343>

Firefighters working on their own can accomplish some things. Firefighters working as a team can accomplish almost anything.

<343>

There is no greater satisfaction than knowing that individual and team effort resulted in the saving of life. This is what it's all about, and this is what makes it all worthwhile.

<343>

CPR and AEDs have proved their value, so in the interest of saving lives, fire-service representatives should be out there pushing these life-saving programs in the community.

<343>

As firefighters, we frequently face danger—that's our job. To face it with foolish disregard is not. Things can be replaced—people can't. Chances should only be taken on the fireground when life is in jeopardy, and then only when you've taken all the precautions you can.

<343>

Rubber medical gloves are a must for anyone working on EMS cases. You just don't know what you're dealing with, and there are times when the medical community won't tell you.

<343>

We should all know three jobs: the one we have now, the one we just left, and the one we aspire to.

<343>

Staff positions in the larger fire departments offer broadening and worthwhile career experience for those officers striving to reach the top. There is more to running a fire department than fighting fires.

<343>

One of the best ways to prepare for promotion is to put everything you have into today's activities. Remember: what your future turns out to be depends a great deal on what you do about it today.

<343>

Personal growth in an individual is in direct proportion to the extent of his or her reading habits. Reading is a must for the individual who wants to stay current in his or her chosen field.

<343>

There are specific responsibilities that go with each rank in the department. Fulfilling those responsibilities well is what prepares us for advancement.

<343>

There comes a day when each promoted individual realizes that he or she knows and understands his or her new job. That is the day to start preparing for the next promotion.

<343>

Each step on the promotion ladder is really a building block, and missing or skipping a level tends to weaken the end product. What we learn at each level prepares us for the next.

<343>

Your Mission Statement should be clear, concise, and known to all. "All" includes the public you serve as well as your firefighters.

<343>

Continuously keep the public informed about what your department is doing. In the absence of information from you, they can only speculate, and speculate they will.

<343>

Discourtesy to the public is not only a disservice to them but also to you and to your department. One momentary lapse in judgment can take a very long time to undo.

<343>

Never, ever participate in a press conference or briefing without first doing your homework! There is simply no substitute for preparation in this area.

<343>

When dealing with the press, consider that everything you say is on the record. In that way there won't be any surprises when the story appears in the paper or the broadcast is aired.

<343>

Clean and neat personnel, sparkling apparatus and equipment, and shipshape stations sends the message, "This unit is ready to go and fully prepared to carry out its role and responsibilities."

<343>

It's a good thing for a Rookie or Probie to remember that his or her reputation within the department begins the very first day on the job. There are few things more difficult than changing one's reputation once it's been established.

<343>

It is a firefighter's task to make order out of chaos, to return normality to the abnormal, and to do this on a routine basis. Few professions are more demanding.

<343>

Just being a firefighter is reason enough to be proud. Being a dutiful and dedicated firefighter is justification for that pride. Never underestimate pride's value. Proud firefighters will give that extra effort that frequently makes the difference between life and death.

<343>

We should be proud of our status as firefighters. A lot of good people have paid dearly to purchase that golden reputation we all enjoy today. The ideal firefighter has an attitude to serve, a desire to contribute, and a willingness to go that extra step.

<343>

It is being proud of what you do and the knowledge that you make a difference that makes firefighting so much more than just a job. It is, in fact, a calling.

<343>

Courage is digging deep into yourself and hanging on when it would be much easier to back out. This is not only true on the fireground, but in many other life situations as well.

<343>

There is nothing wrong with fear or being afraid. Fear is often the parent of prudent action and thoughtful effort.

<343>

When a fellow firefighter pays the supreme sacrifice, we all know deep inside that a second sooner, a minute later, an inch closer, or a foot to the right or left and it could have been us. That's quite a burden to live with, but live with it we must.

<343>

It's not pay status that makes a firefighter a professional. It's what is in his or her heart and how well he or she has prepared himself or herself for the task at hand.

<343>

The officer or firefighter who accepts a gratuity for their service are selling themselves and their department short. If someone wants to show thanks for our service, there are any number of other ways to do so.

<343>

When an individual firefighter's honesty or integrity is compromised, the whole department suffers.

<343>

Do all you can to make sure that you do not wake on some future morning and think, "I should have …" Regret of this nature is tragedy in its purest form.

<343>

You must understand the price you are willing to pay for advancement. When attained, some things are not worth what we paid; many others are, however.

<343>

Give the boss the respect and courtesy his or her position merits. The shoe might be on the other foot one day. If you don't respect the person, respect the position.

<343>

There is nothing inherently wrong with ambition. It is only when it becomes all-consuming or skews judgment that it must be reined in. Loyalty to the department and those that lead it is important.

<343>

Ending Remarks

What you have just read, scanned, or reviewed is a distillation of a good portion of what I have absorbed over my twenty-eight-year fire-service career. As I mentioned earlier in this offering, some lessons were hard learned, others were not so hard, but all came from the stern and unforgiving school of practical experience. If what I have presented here strikes a receptive note with you or helps you in your own fire-service work experience, I feel I have accomplished what I intended from the outset. I believe it is more important to light one lamp than to let others grope in the darkness looking for answers. I hope that is what I have done here. Also, as I mentioned before, I love the American fire service and trust I have not let it down. In sharing this material, I hope I have helped further enhance its luster.

I wish you, the reader, good luck, much success in your chosen career, and may whomever or whatever it is you might believe in keep you safe as you work the streets of your community, saving lives and protecting property.

W. C. R.

About the Author

William C. Richmond spent twenty-eight years in the Philadelphia Fire Department where he held every rank rising from Fire Fighter Recruit to Fire Commissioner; head of that department. He served in both line and staff positions and as Commissioner commanded some of Philadelphia's most noted fires including Harrison Court, the Second MOVE Confrontation, Chevron Refinery and the Coral Street Fire that resulted in ten fire deaths and led to residential smoke detector legislation.

After retiring he worked thirteen years with a local law firm where he coordinated the investigation of major fire losses and other disasters. He is presently a Senior Management Consultant for TriData Corporation in Arlington, VA where he has participated in forty plus studies and/or evaluations of fire departments in twenty states, the District of Columbia and Canada.

He has had published over sixty articles on fire service management, training and operations as well as contributing two articles to *Firehouse Magazine* on the "Second MOVE Confrontation" and the "Rising Sun Baptist Church Fire".

He has lectured at the graduate and under graduate levels at Saint Joseph's University and Holy Family University on numerous occasions as well as at a number of fire related seminars.

Mr. Richmond makes his home in the Philadelphia area and is now semi-retired.

978-0-595-47006-8
0-595-47006-8

Printed in the United States
203738BV00001B/103-114/A

9 780595 470068